QUEER HISTORY A to Z

100 Years of LGBTQ+ Activism

Written by Robin Stevenson
Illustrated by Vivian Rosas

KIDS CAN PRESS

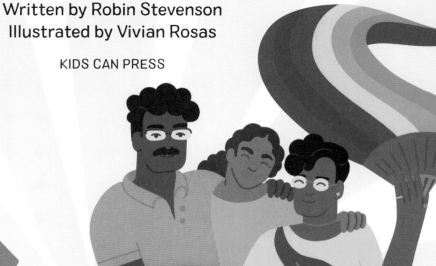

This book is dedicated to all the courageous young activists joining
this long fight for justice, equality and inclusion — R.S.

To the folks who came before us and to the youth ahead who feel different
and are fighting to be seen and heard, thank you — V.R.

ACKNOWLEDGMENTS

Many thanks to Katie Scott, who was not only an astute and reflective editor
but also a delight to work with, and to Veronica Vega and Ronkwahrhakónha Dube
for their insightful and thoughtful feedback during the writing process. Thanks also to
the rest of the crew at Kids Can Press — it takes a team to create a book and help it find
readers, and I so appreciate everyone's efforts. And to my endlessly supportive family
and friends: thank you. I am so lucky and so very grateful to you all.

Published in Canada and the U.S. by Kids Can Press Ltd.
25 Dockside Drive, Toronto, ON M5A 0B5

Kids Can Press is a Corus Entertainment Inc. company
www.kidscanpress.com

The artwork in this book was rendered digitally.
The text is set in Colby.

Edited by Katie Scott
Designed by Barb Kelly

Printed and bound in Shenzhen, China,
in 10/2023 by C & C Offset

CM 24 0987654321

Library and Archives Canada Cataloguing in Publication

Title: Queer history A to Z: 100 years of LGBTQ+ activism /
written by Robin Stevenson; illustrated by Vivian Rosas
Names: Stevenson, Robin, 1968– author. | Rosas, Vivian,
illustrator.
Description: Includes bibliographical references and index
Identifiers: Canadiana 20230448070 | ISBN 9781525308352
(hardcover)
Subjects: LCSH: Sexual minority activists — History —
Juvenile literature. |
LCSH: Gay rights — History — Juvenile literature
Classification: LCC HQ76.5 .S74 2024 | DDC j306.76/6 —
dc23

Kids Can Press gratefully acknowledges that the land on
which our office is located is the traditional territory of
many nations, including the Mississaugas of the Credit,
the Anishnabeg, the Chippewa, the Haudenosaunee and
the Wendat peoples, and is now home to many diverse
First Nations, Inuit and Métis peoples.

We thank the Government of Ontario, through Ontario
Creates and the Ontario Arts Council; the Canada Council
for the Arts; and the Government of Canada for their
financial support of our publishing activity.

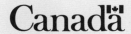

CONTENTS

INTRODUCTION:
Queer Has Always Been Here 4

A Is for
Activism 6

B Is for
Bayard Rustin 8

C Is for
Coming Out 10

D Is for
Drag Culture 12

E Is for
Ernestine Eckstein 14

F Is for
Flags 16

G Is for
"Gay Is Good" 18

H Is for
Homophile Movement 19

I Is for
Indigiqueer 20

J Is for
Jazz Jennings 22

K Is for
Kiss to Resist 23

L Is for
LGBTQ+ 24

M Is for
Marsha P. Johnson 26

N Is for
National March on
Washington for Lesbian
and Gay Rights 28

O Is for
Oscar Wilde
Memorial Bookshop 30

P Is for
Pride 32

Q Is for
Queer 34

R Is for
Raids and Riots 36

S Is for
Stonewall Inn 38

T Is for
Transgender
Liberation Movement 40

U Is for
Urvashi Vaid 42

V Is for
Village Voice 43

W Is for
"We Demand" 44

X Is for
Censorship 46

Y Is for
Youth Activism 48

Z Is for
Zap 50

More Queer Activists 52

A Hundred Years
of Queer Activism 58

Glossary 60

LGBTQ+ Resources
for Young Readers 62

Author's Selected Sources 62

Index 64

Introduction

Queer Has Always Been Here

The history of queer people stretches back a long time because queer folks have always existed. They haven't always been called *queer* or *gay* or *lesbian* or *transgender* — those words are relatively new. But in every country, every culture and every century, there have been men who loved men, women who loved women and people who experienced and expressed their sexuality and gender in many ways.

Before the gay liberation movement of the 1970s, most queer people in North America had to hide their identities and romantic relationships or risk going to jail, losing their jobs or being rejected by their friends and families. Ideas about sexuality were rigid and so were laws: being in a relationship with someone of the same sex was illegal, viewed as morally wrong and even classified as a mental illness. Ideas about gender were equally rigid. In police raids on gay bars, many men, transgender women and drag queens were arrested for wearing dresses. Women were required to wear at least three pieces of "feminine" clothing — this was known as the "three-article rule," and although it was never a formal law, the police used it to arrest many people. Despite the risks, there were some queer folks who refused to hide their sexuality and gender identities because denying their truth also did harm.

In many parts of the world today, these ideas about sexuality and gender are still a reality, and the fight for freedom and equality of queer people is just beginning. In North America, queerness is far more widely accepted than it was in the past, and LGBTQ+ people have more legal rights. That's largely thanks to the waves of activism that have driven progress toward LGBTQ+ equality over the last hundred years. In these pages, you will read about queer history in North America and meet some of the people who led the way, learn about the events that created change and discover some of the places where history was made.

Words Are Powerful

The terms *queer* and *LGBTQ+* (Lesbian, Gay, Bisexual, Transgender, Queer and more identities) are used to describe a wide community of people who are attracted to the same gender or to multiple genders, or whose gender identity does not match their sex assigned at birth. A person's sex refers to whether they were considered to be a boy or a girl when they were born. Their gender identity is their inner sense of being male, female or another gender, for example, nonbinary or genderqueer. *Queer* and *LGBTQ+* are relatively recent terms. In this book, we'll sometimes use them when discussing historical events, even if they aren't the words that would have been used at the time. We do so to avoid outdated language, to be inclusive and to reflect the diverse identities that have always been a part of this community.

To read more about the history of the term *queer*, turn to page 34.

A Is for Activism

Activists are people who stand up for what they believe in, whether that's protecting people's rights, animal welfare or the environment. They work to change laws, educate people, influence public opinion and organize others to join their cause.

In relation to human history, queer activism — or fighting for the rights of LGBTQ+ people — is relatively recent. While the first gay rights group in North America began about a hundred years ago, in 1924, it wasn't until after World War II that the gay rights movement gained momentum. During the war, many gay men and lesbians left their small hometowns to join the military — and for some, it was the first time they met others like themselves, fell in love and had romantic relationships. After the war, many chose to live in large cities, where they could build community, meet in underground gay bars and gather in secret social groups.

As lesbians and gay men shared their experiences of oppression, some decided to fight for change. In 1965, picketers outside the White House and Independence Hall in Philadelphia protested their lack of legal rights. They wanted other Americans to know that they were being discriminated against and denied jobs and housing. A year later, a group of gay men held the first "sip-in" at Julius' Bar in New York City, where the law forbade bars from serving gay customers. They sat down, announced that they were gay and were promptly denied service. This was exactly what they wanted: it meant they could challenge the law in court. It was the first gay rights protest of its kind and was inspired by the lunch counter sit-ins of Black activists in the 1960s.

After the Stonewall riots in 1969, new activist groups formed. The Gay Liberation Front and the Gay Activists Alliance began in New York City that year, and the following year, groups were founded in several Canadian cities. There were marches and protests, speeches to large crowds, and letters to politicians and newspapers. These collective efforts in the 1970s became known as the gay liberation movement. Over the decades, activists have focused on different goals: fighting homophobia (fear and hatred of gay, lesbian and bisexual people, and discrimination based on harmful beliefs about them), funding HIV/AIDS treatment and research, changing immigration laws for same-sex couples, gaining protection from discrimination, legalizing same-sex marriage, protecting the rights of transgender people and combating transphobia (fear and hatred of transgender people and discrimination based on harmful beliefs about them), advocating for fair media representation and much more. The name of the movement has also evolved — it is now usually called the LGBTQ+ rights movement.

These hundred years of activism have created a tremendous amount of progress. Although there are still obstacles to overcome, there are also many victories to celebrate.

> " BURST DOWN THOSE CLOSET DOORS ONCE AND FOR ALL, AND STAND UP AND START TO FIGHT. "
> — Harvey Milk

MY BODY MY RULES

QUEER SOLIDARITY

PROTECT TRANS KIDS

BLACK TRANS LIVES MATTER

Skip ahead to page 38 to read about the Stonewall riots, one of the most famous events in LGBTQ+ history.

B

Is for
Bayard Rustin
1912–1987

Many of the early gay rights activists were inspired by the Black activists of the Civil Rights Movement. This was a time of protest in the 1950s and 1960s in the United States when people fought for equal rights for Black people and an end to racial segregation (*racial segregation* means the separation or exclusion of Black people in public spaces). One of the most important architects of that movement was a gay Black pacifist named Bayard Rustin.

Bayard chose to live as an openly gay man at a time when this came with great personal risks. In 1953, he was imprisoned under a law that targeted gay people. He served 50 days in jail. This arrest damaged his reputation, and many people were reluctant to be associated with him. As a result, much of his work as a civil rights leader was behind the scenes — including his role mentoring one of the movement's greatest leaders, Martin Luther King Jr., and organizing the pivotal 1963 March on Washington for Jobs and Freedom.

Bayard's refusal to hide his sexuality was a courageous act and was, in itself, a form of activism. Bayard later said that his reasons for being out as a gay man were connected to his experiences as a Black man: he knew that standing up for equality and protesting injustice could help raise awareness and educate people about inequality.

When Bayard was 65 years old, he fell in love with a man named Walter Naegle. Marriage wasn't yet legal for gay couples in America. So in 1982, Bayard legally adopted Walter! It was the only way they could be recognized as family, and it gave their relationship some protection: if one of them fell ill, for example, the other would be allowed to visit them in the hospital.

Bayard and Walter were involved in the gay rights movement right up until Bayard's death in 1987, and Bayard's legacy continued long after that. In 2013, Barack Obama posthumously awarded Bayard the Presidential Medal of Freedom to honor his fight for equal rights for both Black and gay people. In 2020, nearly 70 years after his arrest, Bayard's criminal conviction was overturned.

" WE NEED, IN EVERY COMMUNITY, A GROUP OF ANGELIC TROUBLEMAKERS. "

– Bayard Rustin

Walter and Bayard

C
Is for
Coming Out

Coming out means telling people about your sexual orientation or gender identity. The expression is short for "coming out of the closet," a phrase that refers to how LGBTQ+ people have often had to hide their identities to stay safe.

In 1867, German activist Karl Heinrich Ulrichs became the first person to publicly come out when he gave the world's first gay rights protest speech, arguing against Germany's anti-gay laws. But coming out didn't gain momentum as a strategy for change until the 1970s. In recent years, many well-known people, from actors to athletes to politicians, have come out, helping to make the queer community more visible and building support for LGBTQ+ rights.

Every year on October 11, more than 30 countries celebrate National Coming Out Day. This tradition was started in 1988 by activists Robert Eichberg and Jean O'Leary. The date marks the anniversary of the second National March on Washington for Lesbian and Gay Rights, a historic protest march in 1987. It's a day to raise awareness of LGBTQ+ identities, to celebrate queer visibility and the act of coming out, and to show support for all LGBTQ+ people, whether they are out or not.

For resources on coming out to your friends and family, turn to page 62.

❝ MOST PEOPLE THINK THEY DON'T KNOW ANYONE GAY OR LESBIAN, AND IN FACT, EVERYBODY DOES. ❞
— Robert Eichberg

D Is for Drag Culture

The word *drag* refers to when someone wears clothing associated with a gender other than their own, often for a performance. Men who dress up and perform as women are called drag queens. Women who dress up and perform as men are called drag kings. Trans, nonbinary and genderqueer people also do drag, and some call themselves drag artists or drag performers. Today, drag has entered the mainstream — you might have even watched *RuPaul's Drag Race* on television — but it has a long and often hidden history.

Some people theorize that the word *drag* derives from *grand rag*, a historical name for a masquerade ball. In the 1920s, masquerade balls were important annual events for queer folks, and one of the most famous masquerades was held each year at the Hamilton Lodge in New York's Harlem neighborhood. Most of the participants were young queer people of color, and drag balls were where they found belonging, community and a chosen family. It was a night where men could dress as women in elaborate outfits, and where transgender people could express themselves freely despite laws that forbade cross-dressing. But once the police found out about these drag balls, they were often raided. Despite harassment and arrests, the drag ball scene (also known as ballroom culture or house ballroom) thrived and spread, creating vibrant, openly queer communities of color decades before the gay rights movement began.

The expressions "spill the tea" and "throwing shade" originated in Black drag culture! Through the ballroom scene, African American Vernacular English (AAVE) was introduced to non-Black queer communities. In recent years, television and social media have brought these expressions into the mainstream, but their history is rarely acknowledged.

William Dorsey Swann (1858–1925)

William Dorsey Swann was the first person known to describe himself as a drag queen. He was born into slavery in Maryland in 1858, just seven years before slavery was abolished in the United States. In the 1880s, William began hosting drag balls in Washington, D.C. Records describe him wearing long silk or satin dresses and lavish jewelry, earning him the nickname "The Queen." When police raided his 30th birthday party, 13 Black men dressed in drag were arrested, including William. He fought his conviction — one of the first recorded instances of legally defending LGBTQ+ people's right to gather — but was sentenced to 10 months in prison. Undeterred, he continued holding drag events for many more years after his imprisonment.

E Is for
Ernestine Eckstein
1941–1992

Ernestine Eckstein was a feminist, civil rights activist and lesbian who saw the struggles for the rights of Black people, women and LGBTQ+ people as connected. She believed activists for different causes needed to work together to effect change.

Ernestine was born in Indiana in 1941 under the name Ernestine Delois Eppenger. When she was 22 years old, she moved to New York City and came out as a lesbian. She quickly got involved with the lesbian rights organization Daughters of Bilitis and changed her name to Ernestine Eckstein to protect her identity at a time when it wasn't safe to be out. She brought to the organization a wealth of experience from her work in the Civil Rights Movement.

Daughters of Bilitis had begun in San Francisco in 1955 with just eight members, including a Filipina woman named Rose Bamberger. She came up with the idea because she wanted a safe space where she could dance with her girlfriend. A white lesbian couple, Phyllis Lyon and Del Martin, were also among the founders and went on to lead the group as it grew and evolved. The name Daughters of Bilitis was purposefully obscure. It was taken from a poem by French poet Pierre Louÿs — that way, if anyone asked, members could say it was a poetry club!

By the mid-1960s, Ernestine had become vice president of the Daughters of Bilitis's New York chapter. At that time, the group was working to persuade doctors to stop classifying homosexuality as a mental illness — but Ernestine didn't think this should be their top priority. What people needed, she argued, was to be around others like themselves. They needed community! They also needed a powerful political movement to end discrimination, so Ernestine pushed the Daughters of Bilitis toward more direct action, organizing and taking part in demonstrations and sit-ins. She saw this kind of activism as a way to educate the public about injustice.

In 1966, Ernestine became the first Black woman to appear on the cover of *The Ladder*, a monthly magazine by and for lesbians published by the Daughters of Bilitis. It was an iconic photo — Ernestine shown proudly in profile. That same year, she stepped down as vice president and eventually moved to California, where she would continue to work as an activist for Black women's rights.

Fifty years ago, you might have asked someone if they were "a friend of Dorothy" to find out if they were gay. This may have been a reference to *The Wizard of Oz*, as Judy Garland, who played Dorothy in the 1939 movie, was a gay icon.

" ANY MOVEMENT NEEDS A CERTAIN NUMBER OF COURAGEOUS PEOPLE, THERE'S NO GETTING AROUND IT. "

– Ernestine Eckstein

Is for
Flags

With its bright stripes of red, orange, yellow, green, blue and violet, the rainbow flag is one of the most visible and iconic symbols of LGBTQ+ pride. The first design was by Gilbert Baker, a gay man, artist and drag queen, with encouragement from gay activist and politician Harvey Milk. The community needed an inspiring new symbol to rally around: "a flag for a Gay Nation," Gilbert later said.

The original Pride flag had eight stripes (including pink and turquoise), and the fabric was dyed by hand. It was first flown on June 25, 1978, at the Gay Freedom Day Parade, an early Pride march in San Francisco. Only five months later, Harvey Milk was shot and killed at San Francisco's City Hall. There was a huge outpouring of support — and an equally huge increase in the demand for the rainbow flag. The flag needed to be mass produced, and the pink stripe was dropped because of production issues.

The following June, the city's Pride organizers wanted to decorate the parade route with hundreds of banners. Removing the turquoise stripe created a six-stripe version that could be evenly divided, with three colors on one side of the road and three on the other. Soon this version became the standard.

The Transgender Pride flag, with stripes of pink, white and light blue, was designed in 1999

1 Gilbert Baker's Rainbow Flag (1978) 2 Bisexual Pride Flag (1998) 3 Transgender Flag (1999)
4 Asexual Pride Flag (2010) 5 Pansexual Flag (early 2010s) 6 Intersex Flag (2013)

by an American trans woman called Monica Helms. In 2017, wanting to recognize the legacy and activism of queer people of color, the city of Philadelphia added brown and black stripes to the top of the rainbow flag. A year later, a nonbinary Portland designer named Daniel Quasar took this idea a step further, developing the Progress Pride flag. This flag takes the six-color rainbow flag and adds five arrow-shaped lines to the left: white, pink, light blue, brown and black.

New flags continue to be made, such as the intersex-inclusive Progress Pride Flag in 2021, to include and celebrate the diverse identities within the LGBTQ+ community.

The Pink Triangle

Before the rainbow flag, one of the most common symbols of Pride was the pink triangle. Its origin lies in the horrific concentration camps of World War II, where gay male prisoners were forced to wear an upside-down pink triangle patch on their uniform. It was called the *rosa Winkel* — German for "pink triangle." The pink triangle was reclaimed as a symbol of pride by the gay community in the 1970s. During the HIV/AIDs epidemic of the 1980s and 1990s, activists from the group ACT UP turned the triangle the right way up, and it was widely used as a symbol of protest and community solidarity. Today, the pink triangle — pointing both up or down — is used as a symbol of the LGTBQ+ community.

> **66** WE NEEDED SOMETHING TO EXPRESS OUR JOY, OUR BEAUTY, OUR POWER. AND THE RAINBOW DID THAT. **99**
> — Gilbert Baker

7 Nonbinary Pride Flag (2014) 8 Philadelphia Pride Flag (2017) 9 Progress Pride Flag (2018)
10 Lesbian Pride Flag (2018) 11 Genderqueer Flag (2011) 12 Six-Stripe Pride Flag (1979)

G Is for "Gay Is Good"

If you'd been at a gay rights march in the early 1970s, you might have heard people chanting, "Gay Is Good!" This slogan was created in 1968 by Frank Kameny.

In 1957, Frank was an astronomer, working for the United States military, when his supervisors found out that he was gay. Gay men and lesbians were barred from working in the federal government, and that included the military. Frank was fired.

He fought back, suing the government in a case that went all the way to the Supreme Court. He didn't win, but he made history: it was the first time a civil rights claim had been made on the basis of sexual orientation.

Frank coined the phrase "Gay Is Good" to fight against the idea that being gay was immoral or shameful. He was inspired by the Black Is Beautiful cultural movement, which encouraged Black people to take pride in the color of their skin and their natural hair. Frank made many important contributions as a leader in the gay rights movement, but the phrase "Gay Is Good" was one of the things he was most proud of. "If I am remembered for anything," Frank said, "I hope it will be that."

GAY IS GOOD

H Is for Homophile Movement

Until the 1960s, the gay rights movement was known as the homophile movement. The word *homophile* has Greek roots: *homo* means "same" and *phile* means "love."

In North America, the first homophile group was the Society for Human Rights. It was founded by Henry Gerber, who had been in Germany during World War I and was inspired by Berlin's thriving gay community. Henry founded the group in Chicago in 1924, and a Black preacher, Reverend John T. Graves, became its first president. The Society published the first gay newsletter in the United States, named *Friendship and Freedom*. Within a few months, the police raided Henry's home, and he was jailed for three days and fired from his job for being gay. The Society was disbanded.

In 1950, a new homophile group emerged in Los Angeles. The Mattachine Society took its name from a group of medieval masked performers; like them, gay men had to hide their identities. The group was started by a young actor named Harry Hay. He saw gay men as an oppressed minority who needed to fight for their rights. Soon chapters of the Mattachine Society began forming across the country. To coordinate these groups, Harry cofounded the North American Conference of Homophile Organizations (NACHO) in 1966. Adopting "Gay Is Good" as its slogan, NACHO organized demonstrations and challenged anti-gay laws.

After the Stonewall riots, the homophile movement evolved into the gay liberation movement, and eventually, into the LGBTQ+ rights movement that continues today.

Is for
Indigiqueer

Indigenous activists who identify as Two-Spirit, gay, lesbian, bisexual, transgender, queer or Indigiqueer have been working for change for many years, coming together to celebrate their identities and relationships, recover and reclaim their history, and support the well-being of their communities.

Before colonization, there was a long history of sexual and gender diversity within Indigenous cultures. Each Nation had its own practices and beliefs about gender, but for the most part, Two-Spirit people were accepted as members of their communities. In some Nations, Two-Spirit people were highly respected, even holding important roles, such as healer, counselor or keeper of oral traditions and songs. Some Indigenous languages had specific words that described these individuals and their spiritual, social and cultural roles within their Nation.

When white European settlers first arrived in North America in the late 1500s, they saw their religion and culture as superior and imposed their Christian values and beliefs on Indigenous Peoples and Native Americans. This included rigid ideas about gender and the belief that same-sex relationships were wrong. The colonizers used their belief in Christianity to justify stealing Indigenous lands and used religion as a tool to destroy Indigenous cultures. Through the brutal residential school system, Indigenous children were taken from their families and forced to give up their cultures, languages and traditions. This practice started in the United States in the mid-1600s and in Canada in the 1830s, and the last residential school in Canada didn't close until 1996. As a result, much cultural knowledge was lost, including traditions of Two-Spirit people, and homophobia and transphobia became common in many Indigenous communities.

To address homophobia within their communities, Barbara May Cameron and Randy Burns founded Gay American Indians (GAI) in San Francisco in 1975. They also wanted to address anti–Native American racism within the queer community, and to uncover and share knowledge about the history of gender diversity in Native American communities. Fifteen years later, the first LGBTQ+ Indigenous organization in Canada was formed. Based in Toronto, Gays and Lesbians of the First Nations (GLFN) offered healing circles, published a newsletter, held drag shows and even ran a softball league! In 1992, the group changed its name to 2-Spirited People of the 1st Nations.

The term *Two-Spirit* was a new one: it had just been adopted two years earlier, after it was shared at the 1990 Inter-tribal Native American, First Nations, Gay and Lesbian American Conference in Winnipeg, Manitoba. It had come to Myra Laramee, an Elder of the Fisher River Cree Nation, in a dream, and it is based on the Anishinaabemowin words *niizh* (two) and *manidoowag* (spirits). Myra says *Two-Spirit* is a complex idea and difficult to define. It is often described as referring to a person with both a masculine and feminine

spirit, but it encompasses a broad range of diverse identities and experiences. The term *Indigiqueer* is even newer, blending the words *Indigenous* and *queer*. It was first used in 2004, by filmmaker TJ Cuthand, as a title for the Vancouver Queer Film Festival's Indigenous/Two-Spirit program.

Two-Spirit Powwow

The Bay Area American Indian Two-Spirits (BAAITS) made history in 2012 when it held the world's first Two-Spirit Powwow at the SF (San Francisco) LGBT Center. A powwow is a sacred social gathering where Indigenous Peoples come together to dance, drum, sing and honor their traditions and cultures. The dances and regalia (ceremonial clothing) are usually categorized as men's or women's, which can be difficult for many Two-Spirit people, but at a Two-Spirit powwow, women can drum, men can dance jingle dress and everyone can be who they are. Two-Spirit powwows offer opportunities for healing, building bridges and helping restore the role of Two-Spirit people within Native American and Indigenous communities. Today, there are many Two-Spirit powwows, but the BAAITS powwow remains the largest, with more than five thousand dancers, drummers and attendees each February.

Is for
Jazz Jennings
born 2000

In 2007, a six-year-old girl appeared on American national television and kick-started a public conversation about transgender children. Her name was Jazz Jennings, and she was one of the youngest people to speak publicly about being transgender. To her, it was simple: when she was born, people had thought she was boy, but she had always known she was a girl. To viewers, many of whom knew little about transgender identities and even less about transgender children, her story was eye-opening. After the show, Jazz and her family began receiving letters thanking them for speaking up and for making other trans kids and their families feel less alone. Jazz, still in kindergarten, was

already making a difference: she was helping many people around the world learn about transgender youth, and she was creating space for more trans people to share their own stories.

That first television interview led to many more appearances and to a documentary about her life on the Oprah Winfrey Network. When she was 12 years old, Jazz cowrote a picture book called *I Am Jazz* to help more kids understand what it means to be transgender, and at age 14, *Time* magazine named her one of the "25 Most Influential Teens of 2014." The following year, she began starring in her own documentary television series, also called *I Am Jazz*. At 15, she led the New York City Pride march as its youngest grand marshal ever and published a memoir, titled *Being Jazz*, about her life as a transgender teen.

As a public figure, Jazz continues to share her story to educate people on trans rights issues, support other trans youth and work toward a world where all transgender people are free to be themselves. "The world will be a better place when we have that freedom," she says. "I think I'm going to be alive to see it."

> **❝ CHANGE HAPPENS THROUGH UNDERSTANDING, AND ONE OF MY BIGGEST HOPES IS THAT OUR NEXT GENERATION OF KIDS WILL GROW UP IN A WORLD WITH MORE COMPASSION. ❞**
> — Jazz Jennings

Is for
Kiss to Resist

LGBTQ+ activists have protested in many ways: marching, picketing, boycotting … and kissing!

In 1976, two men were arrested at the busy Toronto intersection of Yonge and Bloor Streets, charged with indecency and later found guilty. They were each fined $50. Their crime? They had kissed in a public place. In response, a group of local activists organized a "kiss-in." About 20 men gathered at the same intersection and kissed each other. They were ready to be arrested and take the battle to the courtroom, but this time, the police just stood by and watched. The activists had sent their message: kissing in public was not indecent and should not be a crime.

It wasn't the first time kissing had been used as a form of protest. Five years earlier, a group of librarians and activists set up a "Hug a Homosexual" booth at an American Library Association Conference in Dallas, Texas. They offered free hugs and kisses — and when no one took them up on it, they kissed each other! Activist Barbara Gittings, who volunteered at the booth that day, recalled, "Our kissing booth made the point that there shouldn't be a double standard for love, that we gay people are as entitled to be just as open as heterosexuals — no more, but no less — in showing our affection."

In recent years, activists have used kiss-ins as a form of political protest. In 2018, activists gathered in front of the Uzbekistan consulate in New York City and kissed each other to protest the persecution of LGBTQ+ people in Uzbekistan, Azerbaijan and Tajikistan.

Kiss-ins are part of a long tradition of non-violent protest — and a powerful symbol of resistance for a community that has had to fight for its right to love.

Is for
LGBTQ+

L
Is for Lesbian

The word *lesbian* refers to women who are attracted to other women. It was used as early as the 1800s, and its roots are even older: it comes from the name of the Greek island Lesbos, home of the poet Sappho, who wrote of love between women over 2500 years ago! During the women's liberation and gay liberation movements of the 1960s and 1970s, the word *lesbian* became more common as women began using it to talk about their experiences and to fight for their rights.

G
Is for Gay

By the 1960s, people were starting to use the word *gay* instead of *homosexual*, which had carried negative associations for decades. In those days, the word *gay* referred not just to men who loved men, but also to women who loved women and to the queer community as a whole. The fight for equality of LGBTQ+ people became known as the gay rights movement. Today, the word *gay* is often used to describe men who are attracted to other men.

B
Is for Bisexual

The word *bisexual* refers to people who are attracted to more than one gender. The word *bisexual* was first used in this way in 1892, in a translation of a text from a German psychologist. But the word actually appeared a century earlier as a botanical term with a different meaning: plants that had both male and female characteristics. Bisexual people have often experienced discrimination — or biphobia — within the queer community, and it wasn't until the 1990s that lesbian and gay organizations began changing their names to include bisexuals.

T
Is for Transgender

Transgender people are those whose gender is different than the sex they were assigned — or assumed to be — at birth. Although trans people have always been part of the queer community, the word *transgender* is relatively recent. It first appeared in print in 1965, in a book by a psychiatrist named John F. Oliven, who suggested it replace an older word, *transsexual*. By the 1990s, the word *transgender* had become widely used.

Q
Is for Queer

Queer is an umbrella term that includes all the diverse identities within the LGBTQ+ community. However, not everyone in the community identifies as queer. (The best way to know someone's identity is to ask!) The word *queer*, which also means "strange" or "unusual," was used to insult LGBTQ+ people for many years. It was reclaimed in the 1980s by queer folks who were fighting homophobia and choosing to claim queer identities with pride.

+
Is for Plus More Identities

The plus symbol represents many identities, such as asexual, aromantic, intersex, pansexual, Two-Spirit and more (see the glossary on page 60). Sometimes LGBTQ+ is written in expanded forms, such as 2SLGBTQ to include Two-Spirit and LGBTQIA to include intersex and asexual. These lengthy initialisms reflect the challenge of naming a diverse community that includes people with many different identities all looking for representation, awareness and inclusion.

Is for
Marsha P. Johnson
1945–1992

At age 17, with only $15 and a bag of clothes, Marsha P. Johnson left her small town in New Jersey and headed to New York City's Greenwich Village, which was home to many artists and musicians in the 1960s. It was a place that embraced new ideas and unconventional lives, and Marsha had no idea she would become one of its most famous residents!

Marsha P. Johnson was a name Marsha chose herself: "Johnson" was a reference to the Howard Johnson hotel and the "P" stood for "pay it no mind," which is what she told people who questioned her about her gender! Today, many historians and some of Marsha's friends describe her as a transgender woman, but back in those days, the word *transgender* wasn't used. Marsha used she/her pronouns and often described herself as gay, a transvestite or a drag queen.

Marsha arrived at the Stonewall Inn during the uprising in June 1969. She joined in, fighting on the front lines. In the wake of the riots, she began going to rallies and meetings, and helped found the Gay Liberation Front, a new gay activist group, that July.

During this time, Marsha met other queer young people who, like her, had come to New York City seeking acceptance and community. Many were homeless. Marsha knew from experience that life on the street was hard and often dangerous, so she, along with her friend Sylvia Rivera, started a group in 1970 called Street Transvestite Action Revolutionaries (STAR). They rented an apartment and called it STAR House. It was run-down and didn't always have electricity, but those who crowded in found safe shelter and a sense of community.

Marsha believed no one's rights were secure until those rights were given to everyone. As well as fighting for the queer community, she also spoke out about racism, poverty, homelessness, prison reform and HIV/AIDS. Throughout her life, Marsha faced many challenges and was often homeless herself, but she never stopped fighting to make the world better for everyone.

> **" AS LONG AS MY PEOPLE DON'T HAVE THEIR RIGHTS ACROSS AMERICA, THERE'S NO REASON FOR CELEBRATION. "**
>
> — Marsha P. Johnson

STAR HOUSE

Sylvia Rivera (1951–2002)

Born in New York City to Venezuelan and Puerto Rican parents, and assumed to be a boy, Sylvia Rivera was raised by her grandmother. When she began wearing makeup and dresses, she and her grandmother fought — and at just 10 years old, Sylvia found herself living on the streets. That's where she met Marsha P. Johnson, who took Sylvia under her wing, helping her learn how to stay safe.

Seven years later, the Stonewall riots spurred a powerful new wave of activism, and Sylvia, then 17, was involved from the start. But it was difficult: many of the gay activists were white and middle class, and they didn't understand the violence and discrimination faced by queer people of color, transgender folks and those living in poverty. Sylvia challenged other activists to address racism and transphobia, and to recognize the contributions that people of color and trans folks made to the gay rights movement.

Marsha and Sylvia

Is for
National March on Washington for Lesbian and Gay Rights

The National March on Washington for Lesbian and Gay Rights was the first national queer protest march in the United States. It took place on October 14, 1979, 16 years after the event that inspired it: the March on Washington for Jobs and Freedom in 1963, a historic march for the rights of Black people.

The organizers were worried that few people would risk their jobs to stand up publicly for gay rights, but they still reached out, encouraging activists across the country to come to Washington, D.C. Finally, the day came — and so did thousands of people, some traveling from as far away as Alaska, to demand an end to anti-gay laws and discrimination. In the chilly fall weather, they marched from Pennsylvania Avenue to the White House, led by the Salsa Soul Sisters,

the oldest Black lesbian organization in the United States. Some estimate there were as many as 100 000 people there that day!

After the march, a rally was held at the Washington Monument where singers Holly Near and Meg Christian welcomed the crowd with songs such as "We Are a Gentle, Angry People" and "Over the Rainbow." Activists gave speeches about the incarceration of LGBTQ+ people, the gay labor movement and unequal immigration laws. Legendary poet Audre Lorde spoke about racism and sexism within the gay rights movement. Sandy Schuster and Madeleine Isaacson spoke about the challenges they faced as lesbian mothers, and Reverend John Kuiper shared his story of becoming the first gay American man to adopt a child. Organizers sold buttons that

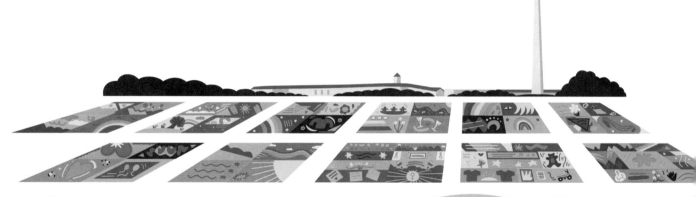

read, "I'm straight and I support gay and lesbian rights." These were for participants to give to their friends because, the organizers wrote, "No minority has ever achieved its equal rights without the support of the majority."

Three days of workshops followed, bringing people together to celebrate, learn, network and strategize. The event drew national media attention, encouraging people across the country to join the fight for LGBTQ+ rights. When it was over, thousands of participants returned home, ready to continue championing equality in cities and towns across America.

In recognition of this historic event, National Coming Out day takes place on October 11 every year.

The AIDS Memorial Quilt was started in 1985 as a patchwork of handsewn panels, each honoring the life of someone who died of HIV/AIDS. It was first displayed in 1987 during the second National March on Washington for Lesbian and Gay Rights. Today, the quilt is the largest community arts project in history, weighing more than 50 tons and commemorating over 110 000 lives.

Richard Fung (born 1954)

One of the activists who took part in the National March on Washington for Lesbian and Gay Rights was Asian-Canadian artist, writer and professor Richard Fung. In October 1979, he was in Washington for another event: the first National Third World Lesbian and Gay Conference at Howard University. Many of the conference attendees joined the march. Richard and other queer Asians marched behind a large banner that read, "We're Asian, Gay & Proud." Inspired by his experiences in Washington, Richard returned to Canada and cofounded Gay Asians of Toronto (GAT). It was the first organization for LGBTQ+ people of color in Canada and a place for queer Asian people to come together, share experiences and build community. In 1982, the group led the Pride parade in Toronto.

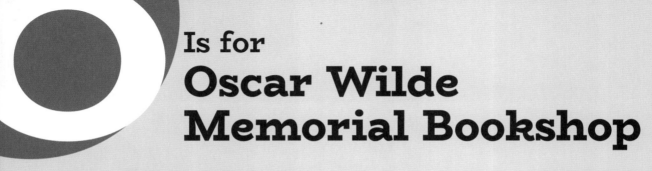

Is for Oscar Wilde Memorial Bookshop

The Oscar Wilde Memorial Bookshop was one of the first gay and lesbian bookstores. It opened in November 1967 in New York City's Greenwich Village. At first, it was housed in a small storefront on Mercer Street, but six years later, it relocated to Christopher Street, just a two-minute walk from the gay bar where the famous 1969 Stonewall riots took place.

The bookstore was founded by Craig Rodwell, who came to New York City from Chicago at age 18 to study ballet. He began volunteering for the Mattachine Society, and unlike most of the group's members, he used his real name. Gay people, he thought, needed to be more visible to help bring about change. When the Mattachine Society turned down his suggestion to open a storefront office, he decided to do it himself. It would be a bookshop that stocked literature by queer writers and a gathering place for people in the queer community. The night before the grand opening, Craig's mother flew in from Chicago, and the two of them stayed up all night putting books on the shelves. Craig named the store after Oscar Wilde, a famous British writer who went to jail for being gay. He decorated the windows with posters that read "Gay Is Good" and "Gay Power."

The store was broken into and vandalized three times in its first year, and Craig received threatening letters and phone calls. But the visibility also worked as Craig had hoped: in addition to selling books and magazines, the store became a kind of community center, with a meeting space and a bulletin board for gay organizations to advertise events. It was a cozy place — there was even a store dog named Albert! Craig started a group called the Homophile Youth Movement in Neighborhoods (HYMN) and began publishing a monthly periodical.

When gay rights activists decided to plan a march to mark the anniversary of the Stonewall riots, they held their meetings at the store. Craig reached out to everyone on his mailing list, spreading the word and collecting donations. The Christopher Street Gay Liberation Day March took place on June 28, 1970, and is considered the world's first Pride parade.

Craig Rodwell sold the bookstore shortly before his death in 1993, and it continued to serve the community until it closed in 2009.

The oldest queer bookstore still operating in the United States is Chicago's Giovanni's Room, which has been around since 1973. Glad Day Bookshop in Toronto, Canada, is even older — it opened in 1970.

Is for
Pride

Every June, millions of people around the world take part in Pride marches, parades and festivities. Pride month is a time to celebrate queer identities and community, and to continue the fight for equality that goes back more than 50 years. On June 28, 1970, exactly a year after the Stonewall riots, thousands of marchers walked the streets of New York City holding signs and chanting, "Say it clear, say it loud: Gay is Good! Gay is proud!" They called it the Christopher Street Gay Liberation Day March, but today, people recognize it as the first Pride parade. That same weekend, groups of LGBTQ+ people also took to the streets and marched in Chicago, Los Angeles and San Francisco.

The following year, Canada's first Gay Day Picnic was held in Toronto. And by 1972, marches were taking place in many cities across North America. Activists began organizing extra events, such as parties, dances, movie nights and sporting events, leading up to Pride Day on June 28.

One of the organizers of the New York City march was Brenda Howard, a bisexual woman who is sometimes referred to as the Mother of Pride. Over the next few years, Brenda suggested formalizing an annual week of events and calling it Pride. At that time, most LGBTQ+ people had grown up in a world that told them being gay or lesbian was wrong, sinful or shameful. Like the slogan "Gay Is Good," calling the event Pride sent a message that empowered people to be proud of their

identities. In 1999, President Bill Clinton was the first president to officially proclaim June to be Pride month.

Pride is now celebrated in dozens of countries. But in many parts of the world, holding Pride events is difficult and even dangerous. In some countries — such as Turkey, Lebanon, Russia, Uganda, Indonesia and Poland — Pride events have been banned, broken up by police or canceled because of threats. Some organizers and marchers have faced arrest and even violence. And yet Pride is an important symbol of hope, and the visibility it brings can help lead to change — and so people continue to organize and to celebrate each June.

Go back to page 18 to find out how "Gay Is Good" became a slogan for queer activists.

PRIDE

PRIDE was also the name of an early LGBTQ+ rights group. In 1966, a group of people in Los Angeles formed an organization called Personal Rights in Defense and Education (PRIDE). The group held demonstrations against police oppression, including one protesting police raids at a gay bar called the Black Cat Tavern, which was attended by more than two hundred people! PRIDE also put out a monthly newsletter that eventually became known as *The Advocate*. Today, it is America's longest running LGBTQ+ news publication.

Is for
Queer

The word *queer* is hundreds of years old. Originally, it meant "strange," but in the late 1800s, it began to be used to refer to men who were attracted to other men. Its first known use as a homophobic slur was in a letter written by John Sholto Douglas, 9th Marquess of Queensberry, in 1894.

Although it was mostly used as an insult, by the early 1900s, the word *queer* was being used more positively by people within the LGBTQ+ community. Some gay men identified themselves as queer, and in 1903, the famous lesbian writer Gertrude Stein referred to two women as queer in one of her stories. Later, as the word *gay* became popular, *queer* was largely dropped by people within the community, but it continued to be used against them as an insult.

Then, starting in the late 1980s, another shift occurred: activists began reclaiming the word *queer*. That means they took back the word, changing it from a homophobic slur to an identity to be proud of! A new activist group played an important role in this change. Founded in New York City in 1990, they named themselves Queer Nation and often used the slogan "We're here! We're queer! Get used to it!" The early 1990s were a time when the queer community faced many issues: widespread homophobia, rising anti-gay violence, stigma and lack of support related to HIV/AIDS, police brutality and stereotyping in the media. Queer Nation fought back, ushering in a new wave of activism and proudly embracing the word *queer*.

Not everyone within the LGBTQ+ community has adopted the word. For some, especially people in older generations, the memories of it being used as a slur remain vivid and painful. But the word *queer* has been widely embraced and is increasingly accepted. It's a powerful word: one that conveys a sense of community and belonging. For many people, queerness means rejecting traditional, rigid ideas about gender and sexuality and celebrating our differences.

Queer Nation created other popular slogans, including "One, two, three, four! Open up the closet door! Five, six, seven, eight! Don't assume your kids are straight!"

R Is for Raids and Riots

In the early 1900s, many cities had secret bars and clubs where gay men and lesbians could meet, but although these places offered some safety in a hostile world, they were not always safe from the police. Special police squads were tasked with cracking down on gambling, illegal alcohol sales and anything else considered immoral — and that included being gay.

The consequences of being arrested in a gay bar were serious. You could lose your job, your housing and the respect of your family and friends. You could be sent to jail or a psychiatric hospital, since homosexuality was seen as a mental illness at the time. Going to gay bars was risky, but it was a risk worth taking for many queer folks looking for community and belonging.

The first known police raid of a gay establishment took place in 1903. The police had heard that gay men were gathering at New York City's Ariston Hotel, so they showed up late at night and arrested a number of men. Thirty years later, the state upheld a regulation against queer people gathering in bars and threatened to cancel the liquor license of any business that served them. But it was after World War II that police raids on gay bars really escalated, rising drastically across the country. They were no longer only about uncovering "immoral" behavior, but about fears of Communism!

At that time, the Soviet Union — a country with a Communist government — was seen as a threat to the United States and Canada. People argued that because gay men and lesbians had to keep their identities secret, they were easy targets for blackmail by foreign Soviet agents. As a result, thousands of gay government employees were unjustly fired from their jobs, an event known as the Lavender Scare. Fear of Communism also fueled homophobia and made being caught in a gay bar more dangerous than ever.

By the late 1950s, queer people were starting to fight back against these raids. In 1959, police attempted to arrest transgender women and drag queens at Cooper Do-nuts in Los Angeles, and the customers responded by tossing coffee cups at the officers. In San Francisco, seven years later, trans women and drag queens at Gene Compton's Cafeteria fought back against cops who were trying to arrest them. As police dragged people outside, a crowd gathered on the street and a riot broke out. This long history of police harassment and queer resistance led to the most well-known riots in queer history: the 1969 riots at Stonewall Inn (you can read all about it on the next page!).

Montreal's Stonewall

Resistance to police harassment is also an important part of Canadian queer history. When Montreal, Quebec, was preparing to host the 1976 Summer Olympics, the city began a relentless campaign of raids on gay and lesbian bars. Then, in October 1977, in a raid on two gay clubs, police arrested 146 gay men. It was one of the largest mass arrests in Canadian history, and two thousand people took to the streets in protest. Public outrage about the arrests put pressure on the government, and in December of that year, Quebec became the first jurisdiction in North America to forbid discrimination based on sexual orientation.

S Is for **Stonewall Inn**

In the 1960s, the Stonewall Inn was a rundown, dirty gay bar on Christopher Street in New York City's Greenwich Village. It belonged to an organized crime family who bribed the police so that they could keep the bar open despite its queer clientele and its lack of a liquor license. But bribes didn't stop the police from harassing the customers who found community at the Stonewall Inn.

On June 28, 1969, at about two o'clock in the morning, police officers entered the Stonewall Inn and began arresting people. They arrested employees for serving alcohol illegally and they arrested customers, especially targeting drag queens and gender nonconforming folks, since cross-dressing was illegal. As the police dragged people outside, the crowd at the inn erupted with anger. Customers shouted at the police. They threw pennies — a reference to the well-known police bribes — and bottles. As word began to spread, more people joined the fighting, gathering on the street outside, throwing bricks from a nearby construction site and slashing police car tires.

The rioting continued until the early hours of the morning and started up again the next night and the one after that. Protestors took to the streets to demand an end to police harassment. The riots brought many people together, fueling the queer community's anger and desire for change, and sparking the creation of new activist groups, like the Gay Liberation Front. A month later, activists held the first mass rally for gay rights, and on the one-year anniversary of the riots, they organized the Christopher Street Gay Liberation Day March, now widely regarded as the first Pride march.

In 2016, President Barack Obama declared the Stonewall Inn and the land around it a national monument. Today, more than 50 years after the riots, the Stonewall Inn continues to operate as a gay bar. The Stonewall uprising is one of the most famous events in LGBTQ+ history. These riots were so pivotal that people often talk about queer history as "before Stonewall" and "after Stonewall"!

Stormé DeLarverie (1920–2014)

Stormé DeLarverie, a lesbian and drag king, claimed to have thrown the first punch at the Stonewall riots in the early hours of June 28, 1969. Some people say that her scuffle with the police as they attempted to arrest her inspired other customers to rise up and fight back. Born in New Orleans to a Black mother and a white father, Stormé was sent to private school after being bullied for being biracial. As a teenager, she joined the circus, where she rode side-saddle on jumping horses. Then she moved to New York City and performed as a drag king with a traveling variety show called the Jewel Box Revue. Stormé stayed involved with the gay rights movement for many years after the Stonewall riots. She also worked as a security guard for LGBTQ+ bars until she was in her eighties!

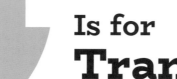 Is for

Transgender Liberation Movement

The word *transgender* (or *trans* for short) describes people whose gender identity is different from their sex assigned at birth. The term came into usage in the 1990s, but trans folks have always existed. Before the 1990s, people might have used the words *transvestite*, which originated in Germany in the early 1900s, or *transsexual*, which was coined in 1949.

By the time the gay liberation movement began, trans folks had been resisting oppression for many years. Transgender activists like Marsha P. Johnson and her friend Sylvia Rivera played an important part in the history of queer activism — but for many years, transgender activists were pushed to the margins of the movement. Many gay and lesbian activists, seeking social acceptance and carrying their own prejudices, distanced themselves from those who didn't conform to traditional ideas about gender.

In 1992, transgender activist Leslie Feinberg wrote a pamphlet called *Transgender Liberation: A Movement Whose Time Has Come*. A new trans rights movement was forming, with activists advocating for protection from discrimination, for more inclusive schools and for access to health care.

In 2014, transgender actor and activist Laverne Cox appeared on the cover of *Time* magazine. She was featured in an article called "The Transgender Tipping Point," which called transgender rights "the next civil rights frontier." Activists fought for representation, and movies, television shows and books began to include positive portrayals of transgender and nonbinary characters, helping to build

public awareness and support. In 2017, the Canadian government passed a bill amending the Canadian Human Rights Act to protect transgender people from discrimination.

This new visibility was groundbreaking, but as is often the case, it came with a frightening backlash: a sharp rise in transphobia. Public figures fueled prejudice by spreading harmful misinformation, and U.S. lawmakers have proposed hundreds of bills attacking transgender rights. In some states, new laws prevent transgender kids from accessing supportive health care or playing sports, or forbid teachers from talking about gender identity in the classroom.

The battle for transgender rights is far from over. Fortunately, a new generation of activists is stepping up, continuing a long fight for a future in which everyone is free to be themselves.

"What Are Your Pronouns?"

Pronouns are the words we use in place of a person's name. Some pronouns indicate a person's gender as female *(she/her)* or male *(he/him)*. Some folks use both *she/her* and *he/him*. Others choose more gender-neutral pronouns, such as *they/them* or *ze/hir*. Today, people are more aware of gender-neutral pronouns and of the importance of honoring a person's pronouns — a sign of real progress. In fact, the *Merriam-Webster Dictionary* named *they* as its word of the year for 2019! Not sure what someone's pronouns are? You can always ask!

In 1970, Zazu Nova — a Black trans woman who had taken part in the Stonewall riots — became a founding member of New York Gay Youth, a group for those too young to join the Gay Liberation Front.

Is for
Urvashi Vaid
1958–2022

GAY & PROUD!

Born in India in 1958, Urvashi Vaid immigrated to the United States with her parents when she was eight years old. It was 1966 — the height of the Civil Rights Movement and the anti-Vietnam War movement — and Urvashi was fascinated by activists. They were, she felt, her people. As a kid growing up in upstate New York, she was too young to get involved. Still, she hung a poster of Martin Luther King Jr. in her bedroom and, unlike most kids her age, she read the newspaper! At age 11, she attended her first protest rally, an anti-war demonstration.

At university, Urvashi found more opportunities to work for change. She came out as a lesbian, and later, while at law school, cofounded the Boston Lesbian/Gay Political Alliance. After graduation, Urvashi began working for the National Gay and Lesbian Task Force (NGLTF), the oldest national LGBT civil rights organization in the United States. She stayed for a decade, becoming the group's executive director and helping it grow into the country's leading gay rights organization. She was the first woman to head a national gay rights organization in the United States.

Urvashi then became an author, and she won the prestigious Stonewall Book Award in 1996 for her book *Virtual Equality*. In it, she argued that there was still much work to be done in the United States to end discrimination against gay and lesbian folks. In 2009, *Out* magazine named her one of the 50 most influential LGBTQ+ people in America to use their voices for positive change.

Is for
Village Voice

The *Village Voice* was America's first alternative newspaper. Beginning in 1955, it published articles about film, music, theater and more. It was based in New York City and became known for its support of the queer community, publishing a Pride issue each June.

But the newspaper had not always been so supportive. After the riots at the Stonewall Inn, it printed a front-page story full of homophobic slurs and harmful stereotypes. Angered, people marched to the *Village Voice* to protest. They didn't have to go far — its offices were just steps from the inn!

Two months later, the Gay Liberation Front (GLF) paid for advertisements in the *Village Voice* to announce the launch of their own newspaper, *Come Out!*, as well as an upcoming dance. The *Village Voice* staff changed the wording of the ads, saying that the word *gay* was obscene. But the paper allowed landlords to place rental ads that specified "no gays" — it seemed that they just didn't want to use the word *gay* in a positive light! So the GLF activists continued protesting until, finally, the *Village Voice* agreed to stop censoring the word *gay*.

The historic events around the *Village Voice* are an important reminder of how the media can shape public opinion and why fair representation is worth fighting for.

Is for "We Demand"

In the pouring rain, over a hundred gay rights activists gathered in Ottawa outside Canada's Parliament buildings, carrying signs and chanting, "Two, four, six, eight! Gay is just as good as straight!" It was Canada's first gay rights demonstration, and it happened on August 28, 1971, the second anniversary of the decriminalization of same-sex relationships in Canada. That had been an important victory, but two years later, discrimination continued, and the activists had gathered to demand change.

A week earlier, they had submitted a 13-page document to the Government of Canada. Its title was "We Demand," and it called for an end to discrimination against gay, lesbian and bisexual people. The document listed 10 demands. The activists were calling for equality in employment, protection of parental rights and an end to discrimination in immigration policies. They also wanted the right to serve in the armed forces. And they wanted human rights legislation to ensure the same freedoms for everyone, regardless of sexual orientation.

The "We Demand" speech was cowritten by Herb Spiers from the organization Toronto Gay Action. He intended to read it himself but crashed his car on the way to Ottawa. Luckily, he was all right, but he missed the demonstration. So instead, a student activist, Charlie Hill, read the "We Demand" speech. "Even today," he told the crowd, "Canadian homosexuals are having their careers ruined, being kicked out of their churches, having their children taken away from them and being assaulted in the streets of our own cities."

Over the next decade, new activist groups formed, marches and rallies were held, and more people came out to support the queer community. The "We Demand" document helped guide the agenda, and slowly but surely, progress was made. During the early 1970s, several Canadian cities banned discrimination against gay men and lesbians in their hiring practices. In 1976, Canada ended its ban on gay and lesbian immigrants. A committee established by the Canadian government released a report titled *Equality for All* in 1985, recommending that discrimination based on sexual orientation be made illegal. The ban against lesbians and gay men in the military was lifted in 1992, and in 2005, Canada became the second country in the world to legalize same-sex marriage.

Is for ~~Censorship~~

Censorship is when a powerful institution, such as the government or a school board, controls what information can be shared. Throughout history, books with queer characters have been banned by homophobic people and institutions who declared them obscene. Over the last decade, as social attitudes have changed, there has been far more queer content created, but in recent years, there has also been a steep rise in efforts to censor that content. This is especially true when it comes to books for young people.

I AM ~~GAY AND~~ A PROUD ~~LESBIAN~~!

Children's books that include characters who are gay, lesbian or transgender are frequently challenged and sometimes removed from schools and libraries. This censorship sends a harmful message to students, suggesting that there is something wrong with being queer. It can make LGBTQ+ youth feel invisible and alone, prevent them from learning important information and have a profound impact on their mental health. And censorship doesn't just hurt LGBTQ+ students — when books are banned, teachers lose access to educational resources, schools become less inclusive and all students lose opportunities to learn.

Students and teachers can also face direct censorship of their freedom of expression. In some schools, for example, they are not allowed to wear T-shirts or buttons supporting LGBTQ+ rights. In some schools, Gay-Straight Alliances have been forced to remove the word *gay* from their name — or have been banned entirely. Some states even have laws that forbid teachers from discussing lesbian, gay or bisexual people or topics in a positive way. And it's not just queer stories and writers being attacked: books written by or about people of color are also a frequent target.

Many young people are fighting back, standing up for their freedom to read and their freedom of expression. Across North America, students have started banned book clubs to discuss the books that are being challenged in their communities. They have written letters and petitions, spoken at school board meetings and protested outside their schools. Librarians and teachers are fighting back, too, standing up for everyone's freedom to read, and of course, queer people continue to write books that reflect queer lives, histories and communities. Books can be banned, but the people they represent are refusing to be erased.

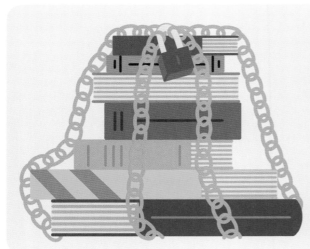

A Banned Books Reading List

Here are a few frequently challenged books with LGBTQ+ characters. You might want to add them to your reading list!

· *King and the Dragonflies* by Kacen Callender
· *Melissa* by Alex Gino
· *Too Bright to See* by Kyle Lukoff
· *Drama* by Raina Telgemeier
· *The Prince and the Dressmaker* by Jen Wang

Is for
Youth Activism

When 18-year-old Elie Lamadrid went to her teacher, Mr. Levie, to start a new school society at George Washington High School in New York City, she had no idea she was about to make history. It was 1972, and no school had ever had a school group for gay students and allies. Elie, a young woman of color, wanted a place for queer students to exchange ideas and advocate for their rights. She got approval to start the Gay International Youth Society, and three weeks later, they held their first forum with guest speakers Jean O'Leary (who later started National Coming Out Day) and Morty Manford. The society created a list of demands, including fair and equal representation of lesbian and gay people in high school courses and textbooks. By 1976, it had twenty members, nearly all people of color: fifteen were lesbian or gay and five identified as straight allies.

Over the next decade, LGBTQ+ student advocacy groups popped up across the United States. In 1988, a straight student at Concord Academy in Massachusetts complained to a gay teacher about the homophobia she saw in their school. Together, they formed a group where gay and straight members would work together for change and called it a Gay-Straight Alliance (GSA). A few months later, students at a school near Boston started their own group, and many other GSAs quickly followed. An LGBTQ+ student movement had taken hold.

Students often had to fight for their right to form these clubs. In 1995, a group of teens started a GSA at their high school in

Salt Lake City, Utah. School officials objected, but the law wouldn't allow them to shut down the club. Rather than allow the GSA to form, the school board banned all student clubs, from chess to frisbee, at the district's public high schools. The legal battle that followed lasted five years, but the students eventually won!

Today, thousands of schools in North America have GSAs (now called either Gay-Straight Alliances or Gender and Sexuality Alliances) or QSAs (Queer-Straight Alliances). They are a place where all students can be themselves, find support, make friends and work for change.

Gavin Grimm (born 1999)

Gavin Grimm came out as a transgender boy during his second year in high school in Gloucester County, Virginia. When some parents complained, instead of supporting Gavin, the school board banned him from using the boys' washrooms. So in 2015, with the support of the American Civil Liberties Union (ACLU), 15-year-old Gavin filed a lawsuit. He spent the rest of his teen years fighting for trans rights as his case worked its way through the courts. Gavin finally won his court battle and has vowed to continue his advocacy until all people can live their lives freely, without harassment and discrimination. He even cowrote a picture book about his journey, titled *If You're a Kid Like Gavin*.

Is for
Zap

One important moment in queer history involved something unexpected: a pie! In 1977, singer and anti-gay activist Anita Bryant was speaking to a room full of reporters about her views against homosexuality. A gay rights activist named Thom Higgins interrupted her mid-sentence by throwing a pie in her face. This kind of confrontation was known as a zap — a dramatic action and strategy to get public attention.

Zaps were often used during the gay rights movement to embarrass public figures who expressed homophobic views or opposed LGBTQ+ rights. Zapping represented a sharp detour from the polite requests for equality made by earlier groups and was directly inspired by radical Black and feminist activists of the 1960s.

The Gay Activists Alliance, a group founded by former members of the Gay Liberation Front, embraced zapping as a strategy. The group formed in December 1969, and their first zap took place just three months later, on April 13, 1970. New York City mayor John Lindsay was attending the opening night of *Romeo and Juliet* at the Metropolitan Opera House when he was surprised by a group of tuxedo-clad protestors hidden in the crowd. "END POLICE HARASSMENT!" they shouted. "GAY POWER!" Over the next two years, protestors continued to zap the mayor in public, until he finally ordered city agencies to stop discriminating on the basis of sexual orientation.

In the 1980s, the HIV/AIDS epidemic brought an even greater urgency to the LGBTQ+ rights movement, and dramatic zaps became an important strategy for activists confronting this new threat. The United States government under President Ronald Reagan refused to acknowledge the devastation. Some religious groups dismissed HIV/AIDS as God's punishment for being gay, which they considered a sin. Fighting for their lives and the lives of those they loved, activists formed the AIDS Coalition to Unleash Power (ACT UP) in 1987. They organized protests on Wall Street, chained themselves to politicians' desks and scattered ashes of those who had died of HIV/AIDS on the White House lawn. They targeted drug companies and the Food and Drug Administration (FDA) to demand access to experimental HIV/AIDS drugs, chanting, "Hey, hey, FDA, how many people have you killed today?"

More than half a century after the Gay Activists Alliance's first zap, we owe a great deal to these courageous queer activists of the past. Today's activists carry on their legacy as they continue to find creative ways to get their message across in the fight for equality.

Activist Marty Robinson, who led the 1970 zap at the Metroplitan Opera House, became known as "Mr. Zap"!

MORE Queer Activists

Aimee Stephens (1960–2020) was a white transgender woman who fought for the rights of transgender people in the United States. In 2013, she was fired from her job as a funeral director after she told her employer that she was transitioning and would be coming to work dressed in appropriate women's business attire. She sued, launching what would become the first major transgender rights case heard by the Supreme Court. In a historic decision in 2020, the court ruled that gay, lesbian and transgender employees are protected from discrimination.

Andrea Jenkins (born 1961) is a queer, bisexual transgender activist and award-winning writer, poet and performance artist. Working as curator of the Transgender Oral History Project at the University of Minnesota, Andrea recorded hundreds of hours of conversations with transgender people sharing their stories. In 2017, she was elected to Minneapolis City Council, making her the first Black transgender woman elected to public office in the United States. In June 2020, the online magazine *Queerty* named her among 50 heroes leading the nation toward equality and acceptance for all.

Audre Lorde (1934–1992) was a civil rights activist, writer, librarian and LGBTQ+ activist. She described herself as "black, lesbian, mother, warrior, poet." She was one of the speakers at the 1979 National March on Washington for Lesbian and Gay Rights and wrote many powerful and influential essays about race, gender, class and sexuality. Audre often challenged activists to see their differences as a source of strength, rather than letting them divide the community.

"There is no such thing as a single-issue struggle because we do not live single-issue lives."
— Audre Lorde

Barbara May Cameron (1954–2002) was a lesbian activist, Two-Spirit leader, artist and community organizer. A Hunkpapa (Húŋkpapȟa) Lakota, she was raised by her grandparents on the Standing Rock Indian Reservation. She left home to study photography at the Institute of American Indian Arts in New Mexico, and in 1973, settled in San Francisco. In 1975, she cofounded Gay American Indians alongside fellow activist Randy Burns. During the late 1980s, she became an HIV/AIDS activist.

Barbara Gittings (1932–2007) has been called the mother of the gay rights movement. An Austrian-born white lesbian, she started the New York chapter of the Daughters of Bilitis in 1958 and edited its publication, *The Ladder*. She took part in the first gay rights protest outside the White House in 1965, fought against discrimination by the U.S. government and worked to change public opinion. In the early 1970s, Barbara was one of the leaders of a successful campaign to persuade the American Psychiatric Association to stop classifying homosexuality as a mental disorder.

The Brunswick Four were four white lesbians from Canada: Adrienne Potts, Pat Murphy, Sue Wells and Lamar Van Dyke. On January 5, 1974, they were at an open mic night at a Toronto bar called the Brunswick House when they sang the 1950s Broadway tune "I Enjoy Being a Girl" with their own original, and clearly queer, lyrics! The manager asked them to leave, and when they refused, they were arrested and assaulted by police. The trial was widely publicized, and media coverage helped spur gay activism in Canada.

Cheri DiNovo (born 1950) is a white bisexual woman, United Church minister and former Canadian politician. When she was 20, she was the only woman to sign her name to the groundbreaking "We Demand" document, which called for equal rights for gay men and lesbians in Canada. As a minister, she performed one of Canada's first registered same-sex marriages — four years before this was legal. And as a politician, she successfully passed numerous LGBTQ+ rights bills. In 2021, Cheri published her memoir *The Queer Evangelist*.

Chris Morrissey (born 1942) is a leader in the Canadian movement to help LGBTQ+ immigrants and refugees settle. A white lesbian, Chris began focusing on LGBTQ+ immigration issues when she and her Irish partner Bridget Coll wanted to live together in Canada. At that time, immigration laws did not consider same-sex couples as family — so in 1992, Chris cofounded the Lesbian and Gay Immigration Task Force (LEGIT), which helped persuade the government to allow Canadians to sponsor same-sex partners. Eight years later, Chris helped start Rainbow Refuge to support LGBTQ+ people seeking refuge in Canada.

Chrystos (born 1946) is a Native American poet, lesbian and Two-Spirit activist from the Menominee Indian Tribe of Wisconsin. Their poetry explores Native American identity, feminism and social justice issues, as well as their childhood experience of sexual abuse and mental health issues. Chrystos has won numerous awards for their writing, including the Audre Lorde International Poetry Competition and the Sappho Award of Distinction from the Astraea Lesbian Foundation for Justice.

Drago Renteria (born 1967) is an activist, educator, photographer and historian who has been called the Father of Deaf Queer Activism. A Deaf Chicano (Mexican American) transgender man, he became an activist as a student at Gallaudet University. After moving to San Francisco in 1989, he ran the Deaf Gay and Lesbian Center and began publishing the first national magazine for the deaf queer community. Since 1995, he has been the executive director of an online organization he founded: the Deaf Queer Resource Center (DQRC). Drago started the DQRC to provide support, information and education, increase the visibility of the deaf queer community and record deaf LGBTQ+ history.

Essex Hemphill (1957–1995) was a poet, spoken word artist and activist. He began writing poems at age 14 and went on to write and edit some of the most important books of poetry about being gay and Black. Essex spoke out about racism in the gay community and demanded that people in the Black community be more accepting of LGBTQ+ folks. He also wrote and spoke about the devastation of HIV/AIDS on the communities he loved.

"I love myself enough to be who I am."
— *Essex Hemphill*

George Hislop (1927–2005) was a white gay activist and the cofounder of one of Canada's earliest LGBTQ+ organizations, the Community Homophile Association of Toronto, in 1971. That same year, he helped organize Canada's first gay rights demonstration, the We Demand protest on Parliament Hill. Later in his life, George fought for — and won — survivor pension benefits for same-sex partners. In 2005, he became the first person to receive the Karl Heinrich Ulrichs Award, granted to those who make significant contributions toward LGBTQ+ equality.

Gladys Bentley (1907–1960) was a Black lesbian blues singer, pianist and entertainer who performed in bars and night clubs during the Harlem Renaissance. Sometimes using the stage name Bobbie Minton, she dressed in men's clothing — a white tuxedo and top hat. She sang popular songs but added her own lyrics and openly flirted with women in the audience, often pushing the limits of what was considered acceptable, especially for a female singer. Gladys became Harlem's most famous lesbian performer, and at the height of her fame, one of the America's best-known Black entertainers.

Gloria Anzaldúa (1942–2004) was a queer Chicana feminist, poet, academic and activist who is best known for coediting the 1981 book *This Bridge Called My Back*. This book, and Gloria's later writing and teaching, had a powerful impact on the feminist movement and the gay rights movement. Her work deepened conversations about race, sexuality and gender, and helped more people understand the complexities of oppression and privilege.

"Knowledge opened the locked places in me and taught me first how to survive and then how to soar."
— Gloria Anzaldúa

Harvey Milk (1930–1978) was a Jewish gay rights activist and community organizer, and one of the first openly gay politicians to be elected to public office in the United States. From New York City, he moved to San Francisco in 1972. He lived in the Castro, an area with a large gay population, and was sometimes referred to as the "Mayor of Castro Street." In 1977, he was elected city supervisor and succeeded in getting a bill passed that banned discrimination on the basis of sexual orientation. Harvey was assassinated at age 48, after less than a year in office. More than 30 years later, in 2009, he was awarded the Presidential Medal of Freedom.

Helen Zia (born 1952) is a Chinese American activist, journalist and community organizer who has spoken out against war, anti-Asian racism and homophobia. She was among the first women to graduate from Princeton University after they admitted women undergraduates in 1969, and later quit medical school to focus on social justice work. From 1989 to 1992, she was the executive editor at the feminist magazine *Ms.* Helen came out as a lesbian on a live national broadcast in 1992. In 2008, she and her partner were among the first same-sex couples to marry in California.

James Baldwin (1924–1987) was a Black writer and activist who published many brilliant novels, plays, poems and essays. Much of his work focused on issues of race and racism in America. James became one of the most powerful voices of the Civil Rights Movement and one of the few civil rights activists who were openly gay or bisexual. He wrote about gay and bisexual characters in his fiction in the 1950s — long before the beginning of the gay liberation movement.

Jennicet Gutiérrez (born 1986) is a transgender immigrant activist who came to the United States from Mexico when she was 15 years old. She works with Familia: Trans Queer Liberation Movement, a national group that focuses on queer rights and immigrant rights. Still undocumented herself, Jennicet made headlines in 2015 when she spoke out during a Pride event at the White House, using the opportunity to demand an end to the detainment and deportation of LGBTQ+ immigrants and asylum seekers.

Jim Egan (1921–2000) was one of Canada's first gay activists. A white man from Ontario, he met his life partner, Jack Nesbit, in 1948, when he returned home after serving in the navy during World War II. During the 1950s, he wrote hundreds of letters, essays and columns fighting homophobia. In 1988, Jim applied for Jack to receive spousal benefits through Canada's Old Age Security program. Their application was denied. Even after 40 years, a same-sex partner was not considered a spouse. They challenged the law, eventually leading to a 1995 Supreme Court ruling that protected Canadians from discrimination on the basis of sexual orientation.

José Julio Sarria (1922–2013) performed as a drag queen at San Francisco's Black Cat Bar, where he told his audiences there was nothing wrong with being gay. In 1961, he became the first openly gay American to run for office, getting enough votes to show that the gay community could have a voice in politics. José founded the first gay business association, the Tavern Guild, which provided support for people caught in raids on gay bars, and the Imperial Court System, an international charitable network still thriving today.

Karla Jay (born 1947) is a white American lesbian who joined the Gay Liberation Front in 1969 and became the organization's first woman chair. In 1970, she helped organize the first Pride parade — the Christopher Street Gay Liberation Day March in New York City — and organized a "Gay-In" festival in Los Angeles. She was a member of the Lavender Menace, a group that fought for the inclusion of lesbians in the women's rights movement. As a writer and university professor, Karla has also played a significant role in the field of lesbian and gay studies.

Ken Jones (1950–2021) began his activism in the early 1970s in San Francisco's Castro District, one of the oldest gay neighborhoods in the United States. He worked for the San Francisco Pride committee for two decades, becoming its first Black chair and serving as board president from 1985 to 1990, and helping fund the creation of the Pride flag. Ken fought against racism and segregation within the gay rights movement, calling out the gay bars that refused to serve Black folks. He also played an important role as a gay elder: until his death, he led gay history walking tours, bringing the past to life as he shared personal stories from his decades of activism.

"Why be ashamed of who you are?"
— José Julio Sarria

Kiyoshi Kuromiya (1943–2000) was born in a Japanese American internment camp during World War II and devoted his life to fighting against war and discrimination, becoming an aide to Martin Luther King Jr. in the 1960s. He was an early gay activist, picketing Philadelphia's Independence Hall in 1965 and helping found the Philadelphia chapter of the Gay Liberation Front. When the HIV/AIDS epidemic began, he became a leader in ACT UP. In 1988, he started the groundbreaking Critical Path project, using the early internet to provide up-to-date information about HIV/AIDS treatment.

Li Shiu Tong (1907–1993) was a gay Asian Canadian man and a very early gay rights activist. He was born in Hong Kong, where he attended medical school and met Magnus Hirschfeld, the German founder of the Scientific-Humanitarian Committee — the world's first gay rights organization. In 1931, Li offered to be his assistant. They traveled around the world, with Magnus giving lectures — and the two men fell in love. After Magnus died, Li continued his own research and writing, and settled in Vancouver. His unpublished manuscripts show a man whose understanding of gender and sexuality was decades ahead of his time.

Lorena Borjas (1960–2020) is known as the mother of the transgender Latinx community in Queens, New York. Born in Mexico, she came to the United States in 1981. She devoted her life to fighting for other transgender people, especially immigrants, and helped many people access housing and medical and legal services. In June 2020, soon after her death from complications of COVID-19, Lorena's name was added to the list of pioneers, trailblazers and heroes on the National LGBTQ Wall of Honor at the Stonewall National Monument.

Lou Sullivan (1951–1991) was a white American writer and an early activist who advocated for the rights of transgender men, especially gay transgender men. He was one of the first people to speak publicly about being both trans and gay, at a time when medical professionals insisted that all transgender men were heterosexual. Lou started a support group for gay transgender men, produced a newsletter that was widely distributed, and helped many people better understand sexual orientation and gender identity.

Makeda Silvera (born 1955) is a Jamaican Canadian lesbian writer who, along with her partner, Stephanie Martin, founded Sister Vision Press to publish writing by queer women of color. In the early 1980s, their Toronto home became known as the 101 Dewson Street Collective, an important gathering place for Black LGBTQ+ activists. Many of the city's Black LGBTQ+ activist organizations can trace their roots back to conversations and meetings that happened there.

Michelle Douglas (born 1963) is a white lesbian who became an activist after she was dismissed from the Canadian Armed Forces in 1989 because of her sexual orientation. Michelle had spent the previous two years working for the Special Investigations Unit that investigated gay or lesbian service members — at that time, queer folks were not allowed to serve in the Canadian military. After she was discharged, Michelle took the government to court, and in 1992, the military ended its discriminatory policy. In 2019, she became the executive director of the LGBT Purge Fund, which manages the multi-million dollar settlement between the Canadian government and those who were fired from the Canadian Armed Forces, RCMP and federal public service on the basis of their sexual orientation.

Miss Major Griffin-Gracy (born 1940) is a Black transgender woman and activist. She was born in Chicago and took part in drag balls as a teenager. After moving to New York City, she played an important role during the Stonewall riots. Soon after, she spent five years in prison for robbery and learned about how racism, inequality and the oppression of transgender people are embedded in the justice system. Since then, she has been working to support transgender women who have been incarcerated.

Myra Laramee (born 1952) is a member of Fisher River Cree Nation, in Manitoba. The term *Two-Spirit* came to her in a dream, and she shared it with others, helping many Indigenous Peoples come together to organize and create communities of support. Myra grew up in Winnipeg, where her parents, Mary and Ernie Guilbault, helped found the Manitoba Métis Federation. She teaches at the University of Winnipeg and has done extensive work in the area of teacher education and Indigenous Knowledge.

Pat Parker (1944–1989) was an American poet, feminist and activist. A Black lesbian, she fought for civil rights, women's rights and LGBTQ+ rights. She was one of the founding members of the Berkeley Gay Women's Liberation, an activist group that fought sexism and racism in the 1960s. Later, in 1980, she founded the Black Women's Revolutionary Council.

Peter Staley (born 1961) is a white American gay activist and a leading figure in the fight against HIV/AIDS. After his own diagnosis, he joined ACT UP in New York in 1987. Four years later, he founded the Treatment Action Group (TAG), a prominent HIV/AIDS activist organization. Peter took part in many demonstrations, pressing drug companies to make HIV/AIDS treatment more accessible and affordable, and was arrested 10 times for his activism. In 2021, he published a memoir called *Never Silent*.

"I'm still here. I'm still fighting the good fight."
— Miss Major Griffin-Gracy

Randy Burns (born 1955) is a Northern Paiute and a member of the Pyramid Lake Paiute Tribe. He began his activism as a teenager, starting a First Americans club at his high school in Nevada before moving to attend San Francisco State University. In 1975 he cofounded Gay American Indians with Barbara May Cameron, and in 1987, when the HIV/AIDS epidemic hit the community, Randy helped start the Indian AIDS Project.

Ruth Villaseñor (born 1957) is a Chiricahua, Apache and Mexican filmmaker and Two-Spirit activist. She is a long-time member of a group called the Bay Area American Indian Two-Spirits (BAAITS). In 2004, she and her wife Diane Pfile opened a pet food store, Paws and Claws, which also functioned as a kind of community center where Two-Spirit and other LGBTQ+ activists could meet. Ruth was one of the organizers of the world's first Two-Spirit Powwow, which was held at the SF LGBT Center in 2012.

"There will be victories and they will be joyous."
— Peter Staley

Soni Wolf (1948–2018) was a queer white motorcycle enthusiast and founding member of Dykes on Bikes, a group that has led Pride parades since their first appearance in San Francisco in 1976. Soni rode with the group for 40 years and helped it grow into a nonprofit organization with chapters around the world. She fought to reclaim the word *dyke*, historically used as a slur, and won a court battle to trademark the group's name by arguing that it was a symbol of pride within the LGBTQ+ community.

A Hundred Years of Queer Activism

1924: Henry Gerber founds North America's first gay rights organization, the Society for Human Rights, in Chicago.

1950: Harry Hay starts a gay rights organization called the Mattachine Society in Los Angeles.

1955: In San Francisco, Phyllis Lyon and Del Martin helped found the first lesbian organization, the Daughters of Bilitis.

1957: Frank Kameny launches a lawsuit against the U.S. government after he is fired for being gay.

1959: Trans women and drag queens fight back against police harassment at Cooper Do-nuts in Los Angeles.

1965: Activists picket at the White House and at Independence Hall in Philadelphia in the first public demonstrations for lesbian and gay rights.

1966: Personal Rights in Defense and Education (PRIDE) holds its first meeting in Los Angeles.

1966: Harry Hay cofounds the North American Conference of Homophile Organizations (NACHO).

1966: Riots break out after police try to arrest trans women and drag queens at Gene Compton's Cafeteria in San Francisco.

1966: Activists hold a "sip-in" at the Julius' Bar to protest discriminatory laws against serving gay customers.

1967: Two hundred people protest the police raid at the Black Cat Tavern in Los Angeles.

1967: Craig Rodwell opens the world's first gay and lesbian bookstore, the Oscar Wilde Memorial Bookshop, in Greenwich Village, New York City.

1969: Riots break out following a police raid at the Stonewall Inn in New York City. The uprising galvanizes the community, sparking the gay rights movement.

1969: The Gay Liberation Front forms and organizes the first mass rally for gay rights in New York City.

1969: Canada decriminalizes same-sex relationships.

1969: The Gay Activists Alliance is started by former members of the Gay Liberation Front who want to take a different approach to activism.

1970: The Christopher Street Gay Liberation Day March occurs on the one-year anniversary of the Stonewall riots. It is considered the first Pride march.

1970: Sylvia Rivera and Marsha P. Johnson found Street Transvestite Action Revolutionaries (STAR).

1971: Canadian activists write a document called "We Demand" and hold the country's first gay rights demonstration in Ottawa.

1972: Students at George Washington High School in New York City form the first school group for gay students and allies.

1975: Gay American Indians is founded in San Francisco.

1977: Thom Higgins throws a pie in the face of Anita Bryant, an anti-gay campaigner, during an Iowa press conference.

1978: Artist and activist Gilbert Baker designs the original rainbow Pride flag. It is flown for the first time at the Gay Freedom Day Parade in San Francisco.

1979:: Activists hold the National March on Washington for Lesbian and Gay Rights in Washington, D.C., the first national gay and lesbian rights event in the United States.

1981: In Toronto, thousands of people march in protest after police launch targeted raids on gay establishments.

1987: The AIDS Coalition to Unleash Power (ACT UP) is formed in response to the HIV/AIDS epidemic.

1987: The second National March on Washington for Lesbian and Gay Rights takes place.

1988: A student and a teacher at a Massachusetts school start the first Gay-Straight Alliance.

1988: Activists Robert Eichberg and Jean O'Leary organize the first National Coming Out Day.

1990: The term *Two-Spirit* is introduced at the third annual Inter-tribal Native American, First Nations, Gay and Lesbian American Conference in Winnipeg, Manitoba.

1990: A new activist group called Queer Nation forms in New York City.

1995: Students at East High School in Salt Lake City, Utah, start a Gay-Straight Alliance, launching a five-year legal fight when the school board bans all clubs to prevent them from meeting.

1999: Monica Helms creates the Transgender Pride flag.

2005: Canada legalizes same-sex marriage.

2008: The Coquille Indian Tribe in Oregon becomes the first Native American tribe to legalize same-sex marriage.

2015: The United States legalizes same-sex marriage.

2015: Fifteen-year-old trans rights activist Gavin Grimm files a lawsuit for discrimination after his school refuses to allow him to use the boys' washroom.

2017: The Philadelphia Pride flag is created, adding black and brown stripes to the top of the rainbow flag to honor the legacy of the city's queer people of color.

2018: Daniel Quasar designs the Progress Pride flag, adding arrow-shaped lines in white, pink, light blue, brown and black to the left side of the rainbow flag.

2020: President Barack Obama designates the Stonewall Inn and its surrounding land a national historic monument.

Glossary

activist: someone who fights injustice or works for social or political change

AIDS: *see* HIV/AIDS

asexual: a person who experiences little or no sexual attraction or desire

biphobia: fear, dislike or hatred of bisexuals; also discrimination based on these attitudes

bisexual: a person who is attracted to people of more than one gender

censorship: when an authority or institution, such as a government, blocks public access to information, books or works of art because they include or support particular ideas

Civil Rights Movement (1954–1968): an organized effort for justice and equality for Black people in America that focused on ending racial segregation and discrimination and securing legal and voting rights

coming out: the process LGBTQ+ people go through as they understand, accept and become more open about their gender identity or sexual orientation

discrimination: treating someone negatively because of their race, sex, age, religion, gender identity or expression, sexual orientation, or disability

drag: a theatrical art form that involves costume and performance and has a long history in the LGBTQ+ community

gay: usually refers to men who are attracted to other men, but some women and nonbinary people also identify as gay. *Gay* is also an umbrella term that is used to refer to the diverse LGBTQ+ community, as in "the gay rights movement" or "gay history."

gay liberation movement (1969 to mid-1980s): this term is sometimes used to refer to the gay rights movement as a whole, but it can also refer to a more specific period of radical political activism that saw coalitions form between many different liberation movements during the 1970s

gender identity: an internal sense of one's own gender as male, female, neither or both

gender nonconforming: a person whose gender expression does not conform to traditional societal ideas or expectations for their gender

genderqueer: a person whose gender lies outside traditional binary categories of male or female

heterosexual: a person who is attracted to people of the opposite sex or gender

HIV/AIDS: HIV stands for Human Immunodeficiency Virus. This virus attacks the body's immune system and, if not treated, leads to Acquired Immunodeficiency Syndrome (AIDS)

homophile movement (1959–1970): the first wave of the gay rights movement in North America, beginning after World War II

homophobia: fear, dislike or hatred of people who are gay, lesbian or bisexual; also discrimination and negative treatment based on these attitudes

homosexual: a person who is attracted to others of the same sex or gender

Indigiqueer: a term used by some queer Indigenous Peoples to describe their identity

intersex: people whose sex at birth does not neatly fit into either male or female categories. Their physical characteristics (such as anatomy, chromosomes and hormones) may include a mixture of male and female traits.

lesbian: a woman who is attracted to other women

LGBTQ+: an umbrella term that stands for lesbian, gay, bisexual, transgender, queer and more identities

nonbinary: a person whose gender lies outside traditional binary categories of male or female

pansexual: a person who is attracted to other people regardless of their sex or gender identity

Pride: a celebration in June to mark the anniversary of the 1969 Stonewall riots, a critical tipping point in the gay rights movement

pronoun: a word used in place of a person's name, such as *she* or *her*, *he* or *him*, *they* or *them*

queer: a term used to refer to the diverse community of folks whose gender identity or sexual orientation does not conform to traditional cisgender, gender-conforming and heterosexual norms; also a nonspecific way that an individual in the LGBTQ+ community may describe their personal identity

segregation: the legally enforced separation and unequal treatment of different racial groups

sexism: the system of beliefs that positions women as inferior to men, and the discrimination and oppression of women that results from it

sexual orientation: a person's pattern of sexual attraction, such as being heterosexual, bisexual, pansexual, gay, lesbian or asexual; also known as a person's sexuality

stereotype: a generalized belief or set of beliefs, often rooted in prejudice, about a group of people

transgender: people whose gender is different from the sex they were assigned at birth

transphobia: fear, dislike or hatred of transgender people; also discrimination and negative treatment based on these attitudes

Two-Spirit (*or* 2-Spirited): generally defined as referring to a person who has both a masculine and feminine spirit, this is an identity embraced by many Indigenous Peoples and can include a wide variety of Indigenous identities and concepts of gender, sexual diversity and spirituality

zapping: a strategy of dramatic direct actions made popular by the Gay Activists Alliance, often involving direct confrontation of homophobic public figures and an effort to call public attention to LGBTQ+ rights

MR. ZAP

LGBTQ+ Resources for Young Readers

Books

Bronski, Michael. *A Queer History of the United States for Young People*. Adapted by Richie Chevat. Boston, MA: Beacon Press, 2019.

Caldwell, Stella. *Pride: An Inspirational History of the LGBTQ+ Movement*. New York, NY: Penguin Random House, 2022.

Lamé, Amy. *From Prejudice to Pride: A History of the LGBTQ+ Movement*. New York, NY: Hachette Book Group, 2017.

Pitman, Gayle E. *The Stonewall Riots: Coming Out in the Streets*. New York, NY: Abrams, 2019.

Prager, Sarah. *A Child's Introduction to Pride: The Inspirational History and Culture of the LGBTQIA+ Community*. New York, NY: Black Dog & Leventhal, 2023.

Prager, Sarah. *Rainbow Revolutionaries: Fifty LGBTQ+ People Who Made History*. New York, NY: HarperCollins, 2020.

Setterington, Ken. *Righting Canada's Wrongs: The LGBT Purge and the Fight for Equal Rights in Canada*. Toronto, ON: Lorimer, 2022.

Stevenson, Robin. *Pride: The Celebration and the Struggle*. Victoria, BC: Orca Book Publishers, 2020.

Author's Selected Sources

Books

Bronski, Michael. *A Queer History of the United States*. Boston, MA: Beacon Press, 2011.

Carter, David. *Stonewall: The Riots That Sparked the Gay Revolution*. New York, NY: St. Martin's Press, 2004.

Duberman, Martin. *Stonewall: The Definitive Story of the LGBTQ Rights Uprising That Changed America*. New York, NY: Plume, 2019.

Faderman, Lillian. *The Gay Revolution: The Story of the Struggle*. New York, NY: Simon and Schuster, 2015.

France, David. *How to Survive a Plague: The Inside Story of How Citizens and Science Tamed AIDS*. New York, NY: Knopf, 2016.

Jennings, Jazz. *Being Jazz: My Life as a (Transgender) Teen*. New York, NY: Penguin Random House, 2016.

Jones, Cleve. *When We Rise: My Life in the Movement*. New York, NY: Hachette Book Group, 2016.

Marcus, Eric. *Making History: The Struggle for Gay and Lesbian Equal Rights, 1945–1990, An Oral History*. New York, NY: HarperCollins, 1992.

New York Public Library and Jason Baumann, eds. *The Stonewall Reader*. New York, NY: Penguin Random House, 2019.

Shilts, Randy. *The Mayor of Castro Street: The Life and Times of Harvey Milk*. New York, NY: St. Martin's Press, 1988.

Websites

The Trevor Project
www.thetrevorproject.org
A resource for young people who want to
learn more about the LGBTQ+ community,
sexual orientation, gender identity and
being an LGBTQ+ ally.

The Coming Out Handbook
www.thetrevorproject.org/resources/
guide/the-coming-out-handbook
An online guide from the Trevor Project
that helps youth explore sexual
orientation, gender identity and
strategies for coming out.

Websites

Historica Canada's Heritage Minutes
www.historicacanada.ca/heritageminutes

Making Gay History: The Podcast
www.makinggayhistory.com

Films

France, David, dir. *The Death and Life of Marsha
P. Johnson*. 2017. Los Gatos, CA: Netflix.

———. *How to Survive a Plague*. 2012. Toronto, ON:
Mongrel Media.

Howard, Josh, dir. *The Lavender Scare*. 2017. Saint
Petersburg, FL: Full Exposure Films.

Pride (six-episode miniseries). 2021. Los Angeles, CA: FX.

Schiller, Greta, and Robert Rosenberg, dirs. *Before
Stonewall: The Making of a Gay and Lesbian Community*.
1984 (re-released 2019). New York, NY: First Run Features.

Index

ACT UP, 17, 50, 55
The Advocate, 33
AIDS Memorial Quilt, 29

Baker, Gilbert, 16
Bamberger, Rose, 14
banned books, 46–47
Bay Area American Indian
    Two-Spirits, 21
bisexual, 24
Boston Lesbian/Gay Political
    Alliance, 42
Burns, Randy, 20, 57

Cameron, Barbara May, 20, 52
Canadian Human Rights Act, 41
censorship, 46–47
Christopher Street Gay Liberation
    Day March, 30, 32, 38, 55
Civil Rights Movement, 9, 14, 42, 54
Cooper Do-nuts, 37
coming out, 11
Cox, Laverne, 40
Cuthand, TJ, 21

Daughters of Bilitis, 14, 52
DeLarverie, Stormé, 39
drag, 12, 13

Eckstein, Ernestine, 14
Eichberg, Robert, 11
Equality for All, 45

Feinberg, Leslie, 40
Friendship and Freedom, 19
Fung, Richard, 29

gay, 24
Gay Activists Alliance, 7, 50
Gay American Indians, 20, 52, 57
Gay Asians of Toronto, 29
Gay Day Picnic, 32
Gay Freedom Day Parade, 16
Gay International Youth Society, 48
"Gay Is Good," 18, 19, 32, 33
Gay Liberation Front, 7, 26, 38, 41,
    43, 50, 55
Gay-Straight Alliance (GSA), 47,
    48, 49

Gays and Lesbians of the First
    Nations, 20
Gene Compton's Cafeteria, 37
George Washington High School, 48
Gerber, Henry, 19
Gittings, Barbara, 23, 52
Graves, Rev. John T., 19
Grimm, Gavin, 49

Hamilton Lodge, 12
Hay, Harry, 19
Helms, Monica, 17
Higgins, Thom, 50
Hill, Charlie, 44
homophile movement, 19
Homophile Youth Movement in
    Neighborhoods, 30
Howard, Brenda, 32

Indigenous Peoples, 20–21, 57
Isaacson, Madeleine, 28

Jennings, Jazz, 22
Johnson, Marsha P., 26, 27, 40
Julius' Bar, 6

Kameny, Frank, 18
Kuiper, Rev. John, 28

The Ladder, 14, 52
Lamadrid, Elie, 48
Laramee, Myra, 20, 57
Lavender Scare, 36
lesbian, 24
LGBTQ+, 4, 24–25
Lorde, Audre, 28, 52
Lyon, Phyllis, 14

March on Washington for Jobs
    and Freedom, 9, 28
Martin, Del, 14
Mattachine Society, 19, 30
Milk, Harvey, 16, 54

National Coming Out Day, 11, 29, 48
National Gay and Lesbian Task
    Force, 42
National March on Washington
    for Lesbian and Gay Rights,
    11, 28–29, 52

New York Gay Youth, 41
North American Conference of
    Homophile Organizations, 19
Nova, Zazu, 41

O'Leary, Jean, 11, 48
Oscar Wilde Memorial Bookshop, 30

Personal Rights in Defense and
    Education (PRIDE), 33
Philadelphia Pride flag, 17
pink triangle, 17
Pride flag, 16
Pride month, 32, 33
Progress Pride flag, 17
pronouns, 41

Quasar, Daniel, 17
queer, 4, 25, 34
Queer Nation, 34

Rivera, Sylvia, 26–27, 40
Robinson, Marty, 50
Rodwell, Craig, 30
Rustin, Bayard, 9

Salsa Soul Sisters, 28
Schuster, Sandy, 28
Society for Human Rights, 19
Spiers, Herb, 44
Stonewall Inn, 38
Stonewall riots, 38, 39
Street Transvestite Action
    Revolutionaries, 26
Swann, William Dorsey, 13

Toronto Gay Action, 44
transgender, 25
Transgender Liberation movement,
    40–41
Transgender Pride flag, 16
Two-Spirit, 20–21, 25, 56, 57

Ulrichs, Karl Heinrich, 11

Vaid, Urvashi, 42
Village Voice, 43

"We Demand," 44–45, 53

zap, 50